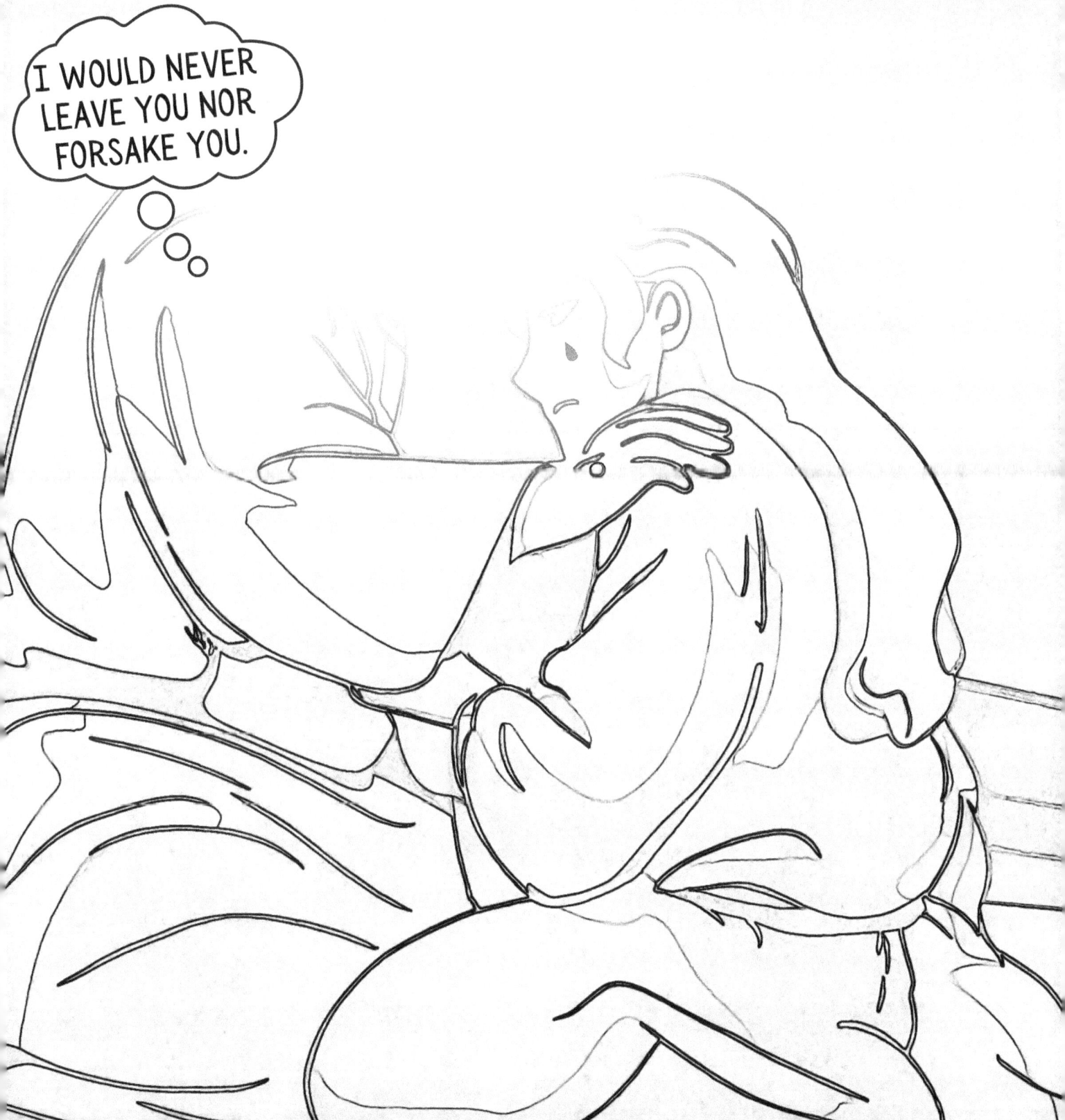

EVEN IN YOUR DARKEST MOMENTS, GOD SEES YOU. HE SEES YOUR HURT, YOUR TEARS, AND YOUR PAIN. DON'T EVER GIVE UP. GOD HAS SO MUCH IN STORE FOR YOU. YOUR JOB IS TO HANG ON, KEEP PUSHING, AND TRUST HIM TO DO THE REST. I BELIEVE IN YOU, NOW IT'S TIME FOR YOU TO BELIEVE IN YOURSELF.

You were never meant to carry the burdens of this life alone. Jesus is the only One who is able to carry them, and He loves you so much, that He is willing to, but you have to take that first step. Pray to Him and tell Him that you need Him. That you believe He is Lord and you believe that He died for your sins and rose again.

And please, never give up. You are so much more valuable than you may ever realize.

If you declare with your mouth, "Jesus is Lord," and believe in your heart that God raised him from the dead, you will be saved.
Romans 10:9

If you would like to know more about Jesus, please visit my website and click on the contact button.
Tm-Ministries.com

Even to your old age and gray hairs
I am he, I am he who will sustain you.
I have made you and I will carry you;
I will sustain you and I will rescue you.
Isaiah 46:4

God never gives up on you, so don't give up on Him.